WILTSHIRE BIRDS

Cover illustrations: front; Black-winged Stilt
back; Kingfisher

WILTSHIRE BIRDS

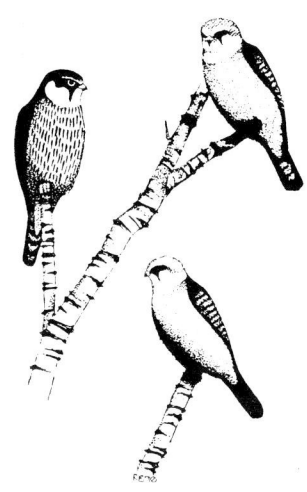

Edited for

Wiltshire Ornithological Society

by

Stephen Palmer

WILTSHIRE COUNTY COUNCIL, LIBRARY & MUSEUM SERVICE
and WILTSHIRE ORNITHOLOGICAL SOCIETY
1991

*Published by Wiltshire County Council Library & Museum Service
and Wiltshire Ornithological Society,
Bythesea Road, Trowbridge, Wiltshire, BA14 8BS.*

Printed by Wiltshire County Council Printing Department.

1991

c *Wiltshire Ornithological Society*

*All rights reserved.
No part of this publication may be reproduced in any form or by any means without permission from the publisher.*

I.S.B.N. 0 86080 223 X

Dedicated to the memory of

John Buxton
(1912-1989)

second President of

Wiltshire Ornithological Society

and

Editor of

The Birds of Wiltshire

CONTENTS

Introduction..4
Acknowledgments 5
Arrival and Departure Dates by S.B. Edwards and R. Turner..........6
Summary of Additions to Wiltshire's Birds by R. Turner...............7-8
Glossary...9
Systematic List by P.E. Castle, S.B. Edwards and R. Turner....10-79
Escapes by S.B. Edwards, S.M. Palmer and R. Turner............79-80
Index..81-84

WORD PROCESSING Miss L.H. Cady
CARTOGRAPHY J. Taylor

ARTISTS
R.G. Baatsen Great Northern Diver, Ring-necked Duck, Hobby and Red-footed Falcon, Black-winged Stilt, Kentish Plover, White-rumped Sandpiper, Caspian Tern, Siberian Stonechat, Firecrest, Hawfinch and Little Bunting.

K.J. Beint Cory's Shearwater, Richard's Pipit and Barred Warbler.

J.R. Govett Black Kite, Avocet, Ring-billed Gull, and Glaucous Gull.

PHOTOGRAPHERS
I.W. Grier Ortolan Bunting.

D.R. Kjaer Black-winged Stilt, Nightjar, Kingfisher, Great Spotted Woodpecker, Reed Warbler, Brambling, Goldfinch, Siskin and Crossbill.

R.H. Lye Water Rail.

H.G. Phelps Treecreeper and Tree Sparrow.

T.M. Pinchen Ruff and Waxwing.

B. Warren Stone Curlew.

INTRODUCTION

Eight years on from the original publication of *The Birds of Wiltshire* in 1981 it was becoming apparent that significant changes had occurred, and were still occurring, in the County's bird population and in the species recorded.

Based upon an idea suggested by Stephen Edwards in 1988, the Executive Committee of the Wiltshire Ornithological Society decided it would be appropriate to produce an update to the 1981 publication covering the ten year period 1980-89 inclusive. No attempt has been made to document the changes in ornithological habitats which have occurred since they were described in *The Birds of Wiltshire*. It is probable, however, that habitat changes have contributed to the decline of some breeding species such as Snipe and Redshank. Climatic variations have also had their effect, causing significant short term population declines (and subsequent increases) in some of our smaller birds such as Wren and Goldcrest. The drier summers towards the end of the ten year period may also have added to the difficulties experienced by the Snipe and Redshank, amongst others.

Overall, eighteen new species have been added to the County list. The majority are passage migrants and it is significant to note that 40% of these have occurred in the Cotswold Water Park. This is indicative of the recent excavation of pits which are ideally suited for use by wading birds and the consequent increased observer coverage.

Changes in the breeding populations have been slightly less dramatic with ten new species being added to the County list, while no breeding species have been lost, although some are getting perilously close to it.

Documenting the changes in bird populations and recording new species in the County relies very much upon the enthusiasm and identification skills of the County's birdwatchers, as well as those visiting Wiltshire. Records from the many hours of census work (such as Common Bird Census and Wildfowl Counts), local and national surveys (Wiltshire Woodcock Survey and BTO Winter and Breeding Bird Atlas), Ringing schemes and the dedicated "local patch" watcher, amongst others, have all been drawn upon. The source for the majority of information has been *HOBBY* (The Wiltshire Ornithological Society's annual bird report).

In *The Birds of Wiltshire* the list was divided into two sections - breeding birds and non-breeding birds. For ease of reference, both of these categories have been amalgamated into one systematic list. The distribution maps at the back of *The Birds of Wiltshire* have not been included or updated as accurate maps should be available in the not too distant future from the BTO Breeding Bird Atlas Survey.

ACKNOWLEDGMENTS

A publication of this type relies on the records sent in by the County's birdwatchers and the comprehensive data available to the County Recorder is due solely to their efforts and enthusiasm. A list of contributors can be found in the 1981 to 1990 copies of *HOBBY*.
 The recipient of all the bird data is Rob Turner, the County Bird Recorder, and it is through his, and his predecessors' hard work and enthusiasm that it has been possible to produce this book. In the last few years, Rob has been ably assisted by Paul Castle in collating records for certain sections of *HOBBY*. For *Wiltshire Birds* they have been joined by Stephen Edwards.
 The Editor and Authors are grateful to Carolyn Palmer for typing the original draft.
 Linda Cady deserves particular mention for her hard work in typing the final copy of *Wiltshire Birds*, for without her assistance and expertise the quality of the finished article would not have been the professionally presented document it has turned out to be. The Wiltshire Ornithological Society is especially grateful to Quantel Limited of Newbury, Berkshire, for their generosity in providing the use of word processing facilities.
 The kind permission of the various artists and photographers (listed on the Contents page) to reproduce their work is very much appreciated. Thanks are also extended to Jeff Taylor for his production of the map of bird sites in Wiltshire.
 Finally, the publication of this book has been made possible by the generous assistance (as a joint project with Wiltshire Ornithological Society) of the Wiltshire Library and Museum Service, through the good offices of Michael Marshman.

WILTSHIRE ORNITHOLOGICAL SOCIETY

Details about membership and activities of the Society can be obtained from the Secretary: Miss Anna Grayson, Westdene, The Ley, Box, Corsham, Wilts. SN14 9JZ

ARRIVAL AND DEPARTURE DATES
by S.B. Edwards and R. Turner

The list below updates Stephen Edwards' *Extreme Departure and Arrival Dates of Selected Migrants (1978 HOBBY)* and is correct to the end of 1990.

Species	Earliest Arrival Date	Latest Departure Date
Bewick's Swan	22 October 1990	26 April 1987
Hobby	6 April 1989	22 November 1987
Quail	17 March 1961	25 October 1988
Stone Curlew	13 February 1953	13 November 1954
Little Ringed Plover	11 March 1989	28 September 1975
Common Tern	11 April 1963	12 December 1930
Turtle Dove	25 March 1970	21 October 1950
Cuckoo	26 March 1968	2 December 1916
Nightjar	5 April 1968	2 October 1978
Swift	4 April 1956	24 October 1984
Sand Martin	4 March 1977	27 October 1987
Swallow	8 March 1989	2 December 1957
House Martin	5 March 1967	3 December 1959
Tree Pipit	26 March 1989	11 October 1953
Yellow Wagtail	20 March 1969	13 December 1970
Nightingale	10 March 1961	30 August 1970
Redstart	15 March 1975	16 November 1980
Whinchat	25 March 1983	28 November 1971
Wheatear	17 February 1965	18 November 1960
Grasshopper Warbler	8 April 1966	3 October 1982
Sedge Warbler	23 March 1957	23 October 1952
Reed Warbler	3 April 1958	23 October 1985
Lesser Whitethroat	3 April 1957/77	30 October 1988
Whitethroat	31 March 1958	24 November 1976
Garden Warbler	31 March 1956	2 October 1965/82
Wood Warbler	24 March 1948	17 September 1952
Willow Warbler	5 March 1959	12 October 1985
Spotted Flycatcher	3 April 1981	27 October 1962
Pied Flycatcher	30 March 1989	6 October 1983
Fieldfare	7 August 1958	23 May 1970/88
Redwing	20 September 1963/81 1982/87	21 May 1978
Brambling	2 October 1966	11 May 1988

SUMMARY OF ADDITIONS TO WILTSHIRE'S BIRDS
by R. Turner

NEW SPECIES 1980 TO 1989

Year	Species	Location
1980	Barred Warbler Cetti's Warbler	Coate Water Coate Water
1981	Purple Heron	Coate Water
1982	White-winged Black Tern	CWP26
1983	Tawny Pipit Sabine's Gull	Colerne Airfield CWP26
1984	Glaucous Gull Cory's Shearwater	CWP68 Woodfalls
1985	Nil	
1986	Richard's Pipit Ortolan Bunting Black Kite	Ebsbury Hill, Wishford Bratton Redlynch
1987	Black-winged Stilt Avocet Caspian Tern	Leckford Crossroads CWP68 CWP68
1988	White-rumped Sandpiper	CWP68
1989	Black Stork Ring-billed Gull Little Bunting	Pound Bottom CWP68 Bromham

NEW BREEDING SPECIES 1980 TO 1989

Year	Species	Location
1980	Common Sandpiper	Steeple Langford GP
1981	Nil	
1982	Water Rail	Coate Water
1983	Firecrest	Shear Water
1984	Gadwall	Clarendon Lake
1985	Nil	
1986	Lesser Black-backed Gull Pied Flycatcher	Trowbridge Longleat
1987	Cetti's Warbler Siskin	Petersfinger Franchises Wood
1988	Nil	
1989	Ringed Plover	CWP29

1990	Shelduck	CWP68

GLOSSARY

All birds recorded in the County are listed with an update, as necessary, covering the period 1980 to 1989. Additionally, notable records from 1990 have been included. The many and varied duck hybrids have been omitted.

The term "during the period" is used frequently in the text and this relates to 1 January 1980 to 31 December 1989.

In the text the species name has been proceeded by a number. This number relates to the page on which that species occurs in *The Birds of Wiltshire*. If the species is new to the County and, consequently, no page number exists from *The Birds of Wiltshire*, a double dash (--) occurs in place of a number. In the tables relating to rare breeding birds, the totals listed are the final totals submitted to the Rare Breeding Birds Panel. These may differ from those listed in *HOBBY*.

In *The Birds of Wiltshire* qualified comments on status were rarely used unless the bird was of unusual occurrence in the County. In this publication, precise criteria for the use of those phrases relating to birds of very infrequent occurrence have been used as follows:

Extremely rare: 1-4   **Rare:** 10-30
Very rare: 5-9   **Scarce:** 31 or more

The use of the terms uncommon and common were based upon the judgement of the authors and editor, and do not follow strict numerical criteria which would, in most cases, have been impossible to calculate.

Where a species has been recorded 20 or less times in Wiltshire, since records began, the total is included in the initial status comment. It is then further split by stating the number during the period 1980-1989 inclusive.

Where a species has been recorded five or less times during the period each record is itemised. Occasionally it was considered worthwhile itemising several extra records.

The list follows the sequence and nomenclature of Professor K. H. Voous.

The following abbreviations have been used in the text:

CWP   Cotswold Water Park - where this is followed by a number this refers to the pit designation number used by the gravel extraction companies and in the Local Authority map for the Water Park.
GP   Gravel Pit
SF   Sewage Farm
MOD   Ministry of Defence
-     In a table this means: no count made or data not available.

SYSTEMATIC LIST

by P.E. Castle, S.B. Edwards and R. Turner

RED-THROATED DIVER *Gavia stellata*   120
A rare winter visitor with 20 records, two of which were during the period.

  3 December 1981: Netheravon - one found floundering on a road.
  1-8 January 1986: Shear Water - one oiled on belly.

BLACK-THROATED DIVER *Gavia arctica*   121
A rare winter visitor with 12 records, 2 of which were during the period.

  24-31 October 1981: Steeple Langford GP - one.
  21 January 1985: Melksham - one found grounded.

GREAT NORTHERN DIVER *Gavia immer*   121

A rare winter visitor with 18 records, 2 of which were during the period.

  1 December 1988 to 1 January 1989: CWP68 - first winter bird.
  19-28 December 1989: Shear Water - first winter bird.

These were part of considerable influxes of this species to the southern counties following severe gales.

LITTLE GREBE *Tachybaptus ruficollis*   63
A locally common resident with between 40 and 50 pairs recorded as breeding annually.

GREAT-CRESTED GREBE *Podiceps cristatus* 64
A locally common resident.

Between 30 and 40 pairs breeding annually on the larger waters. Numbers have increased at the CWP.

RED-NECKED GREBE *Podiceps grisegena* 122
A rare winter visitor with 16 records, 4 of which were during the period.

13 February 1982: CWP26 - two birds.
13 November 1982: Steeple Langford GP.
7 May-15 June 1986: River Avon, Netheravon - an adult in full summer plumage - a most unusual record.
17-28 January 1987: Coate Water.

SLAVONIAN GREBE *Podiceps auritus* 122
A rare winter visitor with 18 records, 2 of which were during the period.

1-4 January 1982: Coate Water.
9-28 January 1989: CWP26.

BLACK-NECKED GREBE *Podiceps nigricollis* 123
A rare winter visitor and passage migrant with 3 records during the period.

26 August 1982: CWP30
11-14 May 1984: Steeple Langford GP - a pair in summer plumage.
6 October 1985: Steeple Langford GP.

FULMAR *Fulmarus glacialis* 123
An extremely rare vagrant with 3 records (one in 1897, 2 in 1978).

CORY'S SHEARWATER *Calonectris diomedea*   --

An extremely rare vagrant with only one
record.

3 September 1984: Woodfalls - one
found grounded.

MANX SHEARWATER *Puffinus puffinus*   123
A rare vagrant with 16 records, 8 of which were during the period.

All but one of the 16 records occurred in September and most followed a period of gales. Of the 8 during the period, all occurred in the northern half of the County. Two were found dead and at least four others were successfully released later.

WILSON'S PETREL *Oceanites oceanicus*   124
An extremely rare vagrant with one record in 1849.

STORM PETREL *Hydrobates pelagicus*   124
A very rare vagrant with 9 records, one of which was during the period.

21 December 1989: Biddestone - an adult found dead following severe gales and a large wreck of Petrels along the south coast and Bristol Channel involving several hundred Leach's but only six Storm Petrels. The bird had been ringed as an adult at Cape Clear Island, Co. Cork on 8 August 1980.

LEACH'S PETREL *Oceanodroma leucorhoa*   124
A rare vagrant, usually during a "wreck". Two occurred during the period.

15 November 1987: CWP68 - a very tired individual, not present next day.
25 December 1989: Stourton - one found dead (see notes after previous species).

GANNET *Sula bassana* 125
A rare vagrant with 16 records, 3 of which were during the period.

25 May 1982: Ashton Keynes - 4 immatures in flight.
16 September 1982: Covingham (near Swindon) - 2 immatures in flight west.
17 October 1987: Bradford-on-Avon - an adult picked up exhausted, later released. An obvious casualty of the "Great Storm" of 15 October.

CORMORANT *Phalacrocorax carbo* 125
An uncommon visitor, but increasing.

Numbers have grown considerably in the CWP (particularly during the winter, with a record count of 56 in December 1990) and on the Salisbury Avon. The species is also regular at Coate Water. Passage birds of the race *P.c. sinensis* are recorded annually in spring. It is possible that the species will attempt to breed in the County in the near future.

SHAG *Phalacrocorax aristotelis* 125
A rare vagrant with 8 records during the period.

A bird in distress at Shear Water 29 August 1982 was caught and examined by a vet. Two leeches were found and removed, one from the roof of the mouth and one way down in the larynx. The bird was returned to the lake and was absent next morning.

One grounded at Etchilhampton on 18 February 1984 had been ringed at the Isle of May in June 1983.

Monthly totals of known dates:-

Jan	Feb	Mar	Apr	May	June	July	Aug	Sept	Oct	Nov	Dec
2	2	1	1	0	0	0	1	0	3	4	4

BITTERN *Botaurus stellaris* 126
A rare winter visitor which is decreasing.

There were 7 records during the period. Since 1985 there have been only two records; at Shear Water and Broad Chalke in 1987.

LITTLE BITTERN *Ixobrychus minutus* 126
An extremely rare vagrant with 5 records (none since 1940).

NIGHT HERON *Nycticorax nycticorax* 126
A rare vagrant with 10 records, 4 of which were during the period and one additional record from 1990.

17 June 1983: CWP40 - a third year bird.
3-10 February 1985: Dinton - an adult.
4 July 1987: Coate Water - a second summer bird.
6-24 April 1988: Longbridge Deverill - an adult.
7 May 1990: Coate Water - an adult.

Escaped birds from the free flying feral population at Edinburgh Zoo have been recorded, surprisingly, both in the Downton area from 10 December 1987 to 11 January 1988 and 10 November 1989 to 17 March 1990. Both were immatures.

SQUACCO HERON *Ardeola ralloides* 126
An extremely rare vagrant with 2 old records (none this century).

GREY HERON *Ardea cinerea* 65
A common resident.

Despite fluctuations at regular heronries, the total number of annual breeding pairs has remained stable varying from 110 to 140 (average 123). Heronries lost during the period have been Britford (1982); Peckingell (1985); Savernake (1987) and Bathampton (1989). New heronries have formed at Longleat (1985), Coate Water (1986) and Corsham Lake (1987). Isolated breeding has occurred at Tockenham in 1982 and Cricklade in 1988. The heronry at Coate Water is unusual because of the low height of the nests, some even being at water level.

PURPLE HERON *Ardea purpurea* --
An extremely rare vagrant with 3 records.

16 May 1981: Coate Water - a first summer bird.
27 June 1987: CWP, Waterhay Bridge - an immature.
1 May 1988: Shalbourne - an adult.

BLACK STORK *Ciconia nigra* --
An extremely rare vagrant with only one record.

26 May 1989: Pound Bottom - one in flight.

WHITE STORK *Ciconia ciconia* 126
A very rare vagrant with 8 records. None of which were during the period.

GLOSSY IBIS *Plegadis falcinellus* 127
An extremely rare vagrant with 2 old records (1875 and 1915).

SPOONBILL *Platalea leucorodia* 127
An extremely rare vagrant with 5 records, 3 of which were during the period.

9 June 1982: CWP40.
13 September 1988: Devizes.
4 April 1989: Leckford Crossroads.

MUTE SWAN *Cygnus olor* 66
A common resident.

The national census of 1990 revealed a healthy increase in Wiltshire, with the River Avon (Salisbury) holding the highest density in the country. The number of pairs actually breeding was low however, due to the drought.

Winter flocks of over 100 birds are regular at CWP, River Wylye and the River Avon (Salisbury).

	1955	1961	1978	1990
Breeding Pairs	117	128	134	102
Non Breeding Birds	274*	464*	384*	591

* *The Birds of Wiltshire* refers to these as non breeding pairs but the figures actually refer to non breeding birds.

BEWICK'S SWAN *Cygnus columbianus* 127
An uncommon winter visitor.

Recorded annually during the period, the majority of records being associated with hard weather influxes in January, while a secondary peak of passage birds has been noted in November.

Number of records per month:

Jan	Feb	Mar	Apr	May	June	July	Aug	Sept	Oct	Nov	Dec
14	6	1	2	0	0	0	0	0	3	8	4

15

WHOOPER SWAN *Cygnus cygnus* 128
A rare vagrant with 20 records, one of which was during the period.
25 February-15 March 1984: Silbury Hill - two adults.

PINK-FOOTED GOOSE *Anser brachyrhynchus* 128
A very rare vagrant with 9 records, 3 (possibly wild birds) of which were during the period. Those birds considered to be escapes have been omitted. *(See also pages 79 & 80).*

13 November 1983: CWP37 - two.
10 December 1986: Stourhead Lake - one.
20-28 December 1986: CWP29 - one.

WHITE-FRONTED GOOSE *Anser albifrons* 128
An uncommon winter visitor which was recorded in most years of the period. The majority of records were in December and January, especially of birds moving towards the Severn in hard weather. Most large flocks were seen flying north over the west of the County.

Number of records per month:

Jan	Feb	Mar	Apr	May	June	July	Aug	Sept	Oct	Nov	Dec
13	2	2	0	0	0	0	0	0	0	3	7

GREYLAG GOOSE *Anser anser* 67
An extremely rare vagrant and scarce feral breeder.

A feral breeding population occurs at the CWP with occasional birds at other sites. It is probable that there have been no genuine wild birds this century.

CANADA GOOSE *Branta canadensis* 67
A common feral breeder.

A considerable increase in numbers has occurred during the period with breeding noted at 6 sites in 1980, increasing to 22 in 1988. A general expansion has occurred in a south and west direction. There has been a three-fold increase of numbers in the County in the last decade as shown by the peak yearly counts for the two major locations.

	1980	1981	1982	1983	1984	1985	1986	1987	1988	1989
Coate Water	135	113	100	119	119	115	130	168	215	334
CWP	-	-	92	-	114	250	370	600	420	550

BARNACLE GOOSE *Branta leucopsis* 129
An extremely rare vagrant and feral visitor.

With two records of possibly wild birds in the last century, there have been annual feral occurrences in recent years. *(See also pages 79 & 80)*.

BRENT GOOSE *Branta bernicla* 129
A rare vagrant with 10 records, 3 of which occurred during the period and an additional record in 1990.

8 November 1982: Boscombe Down - one landed on runway.
21 March 1985: Wick Down, near Salisbury - 200-300 overflew at night.
20 October 1988: CWP68 - four.
31 March 1990: Larkhill - two in flight north.

EGYPTIAN GOOSE *Alopochen aegyptiacus* --
A very rare feral visitor.

One at Great Durnford in March 1982. Since 1988 there has been an increase in the County with a pair at Salisbury and 3 regular in the Swindon area during 1988 and 1989, increasing to 4 in 1990.

RUDDY SHELDUCK *Tadorna ferruginea* 129
A very rare vagrant and rare feral visitor with 18 records, 13 of which occurred during the period.

The status of the earliest County records are uncertain and these may have been feral birds. *(See also pages 79 & 80)*.

The main concentration of records have occurred in spring and autumn. Some of the birds have been associated with Shelduck and could have been from Continental populations.

SHELDUCK *Tadorna tadorna* 130
An uncommon summer visitor, passage migrant and extremely rare breeder.

An increasingly regular visitor to CWP, the main period being January to May with adults disappearing to moult in the summer. Displaying pairs have been regular since 1987, culminating with breeding success in 1990. Over ten birds are present most springs with a March peak. Elsewhere a passage visitor with regular records in spring and late autumn every year.

MANDARIN *Aix galericulata* --
A scarce local feral breeder.

The feral population increased during the period from a single record in 1980 to four breeding pairs, and up to thirty-five birds at fifteen other sites in 1989. This population is mostly centred along the Salisbury Avon, Wylye and Nadder, and is occasionally increased by introductions.

WIGEON *Anas penelope* 130
A locally common winter visitor.

Large flocks occur at CWP and Standlynch every year, with regular small flocks also at Coate Water and the River Kennet. The trend is towards higher numbers at CWP with a January peak, hard winters increasing numbers and distribution. There is a record of possible hybrid breeding in 1989.

	1980	1981	1982	1983	1984	1985	1986	1987	1988	1989
CWP	250	170	-	400	16	400	800	1200	810	369
Coate Water	-	12	-	30	18	84	49	145	17	5
Standlynch	200	170	130	220	220	-	120	500	400	250

GADWALL *Anas strepera* 130
A locally common winter visitor and extremely rare breeder.

Numbers of Gadwall have increased through the decade, the main wintering sites being Clarendon Lake, CWP, Fonthill Lake and Steeple Langford GP. Numbers peak from November to March. Breeding of a single pair was noted at Clarendon Lake in 1984 and 1988 to 1990.

	1980	1981	1982	1983	1984	1985	1986	1987	1988	1989
CWP	-	-	-	-	16	39	51	78	67	105

TEAL *Anas crecca* 68
A common winter visitor and former breeder (last in 1976).

Peak numbers have shown an upward trend at CWP, with birds summering in six of the last ten years.

	1980	1981	1982	1983	1984	1985	1986	1987	1988	1989
CWP	-	-	-	20	157	250	350	305	565	432
Coate Water	150	110	143	108	125	250	134	88	90	90

MALLARD *Anas platyrhynchos* 68
A common resident and winter visitor.

This species remains widespread and common with no real evidence of a change in numbers. There has been a recent tendency towards an August peak at CWP.

	1980	1981	1982	1983	1984	1985	1986	1987	1988	1989
CWP	-	-	-	-	672	237	300	800	850	304
Coate Water	-	-	-	-	-	260	193	293	180	101
Swindon	-	-	-	-	-	-	403	396	345	442

PINTAIL *Anas acuta* 131
An uncommon winter visitor.

An annual visitor in small numbers recorded mainly in the autumn and winter, though of sporadic occurrence. January is the peak month.

	1980	1981	1982	1983	1984	1985	1986	1987	1988	1989
CWP	-	3	-	4	1	18	2	1	4	6
Rest of Wilts	2	2	4	2	4	7	1	8	1	1

An exceptional influx occurred at CWP in February 1990 with up to 98 birds.

GARGANEY *Anas querquedula* 131
A scarce passage migrant.

Recorded in eight years since 1980 with the majority of records from CWP and Coate Water. Spring passage peaks in May with a smaller passage in September/October. Pairs have summered in three years at CWP.

Number of records per month:

Jan	Feb	Mar	Apr	May	June	July	Aug	Sept	Oct	Nov	Dec
0	0	3	3	4	3	0	0	3	1	0	0

SHOVELER *Anas clypeta* 69
A locally common visitor which has bred (1946 and 1972).

Coate Water and Fonthill Lake are regular winter sites with CWP becoming more regular. Peak numbers usually occur in December with a departure in hard weather. Most birds leave during April with a return from August, pairs regularly staying into May at CWP and Coate Water.

	1980	1981	1982	1983	1984	1985	1986	1987	1988	1989
CWP	-	4	-	-	8	10	4	14	22	46
Coate Water	46	47	20	31	20	34	23	18	22	30

RED-CRESTED POCHARD *Netta rufina* 70
A very rare vagrant and scarce feral breeder.

Originally a rare vagrant but records are now masked by a feral population in CWP where numbers have increased considerably over the past few years. During the period, there have been only seven records away from CWP, mostly concentrated in the south of the County. See also Baatsen, *HOBBY 1990*.

	1980	1981	1982	1983	1984	1985	1986	1987	1988	1989
CWP	8	7	5	14	9	12	8	13	24	32

POCHARD *Aythya ferina* 71
Common winter visitor and very rare breeder.

No great change has occurred in the status of this duck during the period. Peak winter numbers occur in November and December with a departure early in March. Most birds return in October though a moult flock of males at CWP begins to form in June.

	1980	1981	1982	1983	1984	1985	1986	1987	1988	1989
CWP	-	130	90	405	230	360	418	550	431	300

Breeding remains restricted to a few reed fringed lakes.

	1980	1981	1982	1983	1984	1985	1986	1987	1988	1989
Number of Localities	2	2	2	1	2	3	2	2	2	3
Confirmed Pairs	6	4	3	1	3	6	7	5	4	5

RING-NECKED DUCK *Aythya collaris* 131

An extremely rare vagrant with 4 records, 2 of which were during the period.

17 October to 1 December 1980: Corsham Lake - female.
27 January to 7 February 1981: Corsham Lake - female. Same bird.
14 October 1989: CWP73 - female.

FERRUGINOUS DUCK *Aythya nyroca* 131
An extremely rare winter visitor with 5 records, 2 of which were during the period.

11 November 1983 to year end: Corsham Lake - female.
6 January 1987: Corsham Lake - male.

TUFTED DUCK *Aythya fuligula* 72
A common winter visitor and breeder.

No evidence of a change in status. Peak counts occur in autumn from August to November due to young birds and moulting flocks.

	1980	1981	1982	1983	1984	1985	1986	1987	1988	1989
CWP	-	40	130	217	156	147	99	300	215	146

The breeding range has remained unchanged as have the numbers involved with a local distribution in the Thames and Kennet basins and, to a lesser extent, those of the Salisbury Avon and Wylye.

	1980	1981	1982	1983	1984	1985	1986	1987	1988	1989
Number of Localities	9	-	9	16	11	10	11	12	12	9
Confirmed Pairs	47	43	40	55	24	19	29	56	35	29

SCAUP *Aythya marila* 132
A rare winter visitor.

There have been 12 records during the period with the majority from November to February, though recorded in every month from October to June. Many of the records relate to hard weather movements.

Number of records per month:

Jan	Feb	Mar	Apr	May	June	July	Aug	Sept	Oct	Nov	Dec
2	2	1	1	2	1	0	0	0	1	2	3

EIDER *Somateria mollissima* 132
An extremely rare vagrant with 2 records from the last century.

LONG-TAILED DUCK *Clangula hyemalis* 132
A very rare vagrant with 8 records, 3 of which were during the period.

5-22 November 1980: Liden Lagoon - immature.
12 December 1982: Longleat Lake - female.
31 December 1982: Fonthill Lake - female (probably same individual as Longleat bird).
1-8 January 1983: Steeple Langford GP - immature.

COMMON SCOTER *Melanitta nigra* 133
A rare passage migrant.

Recorded less than annually with recent records from March to April and July to October. (April and August being the peak months).

VELVET SCOTER *Melanitta fusca* 133
An extremely rare vagrant with 4 records, the last being in January 1979.

GOLDENEYE *Bucephala clangula* 133
A locally common winter visitor.

Numbers have increased during the period as has the length of stay. The only regular flock was at CWP where good numbers occur from November to April, with a January peak. There is evidence of passage in November when the species is more widely recorded.

	1980	1981	1982	1983	1984	1985	1986	1987	1988	1989
CWP	15	20	16	37	25	28	16	40	54	50

SMEW *Mergus albellus* 133
A scarce winter visitor.

Less than annual with most records between January and March, especially associated with cold weather influxes. Thirteen were recorded in January 1985 and nine in January 1987. This species can be recorded on any waters during influxes.

Number of birds recorded per year:

1980	1981	1982	1983	1984	1985	1986	1987	1988	1989
1	0	3	0	2	13	5	9	0	2

RED-BREASTED MERGANSER *Mergus serrator* 134
A rare vagrant with 19 records, 2 of which were during the period.

6 February 1983: CWP - male.
17 November 1988: Coate Water- female.

GOOSANDER *Mergus merganser* 134
An uncommon winter visitor.

Recorded annually with CWP, Coate Water, Edington Lake and Corsham Lake being the main sites. Most have occurred from November to March with a January peak, and some passage occurring in March. Hard weather influxes occur at times with 20 in January 1982, 26 in January 1985 and 22 in January 1987.

RUDDY DUCK *Oxyura jamaicensis* 73
An uncommon winter visitor and very rare breeder.

Records have increased during the period with breeding at Steeple Langford GP since 1988 and at Fonthill Lake and Clarendon Lake in 1990.

HONEY BUZZARD *Pernis apivorus* 134
A rare passage migrant which has summered.

BLACK KITE *Milvus migrans*

An extremely rare vagrant with only one record.

12 June 1986: Redlynch.

RED KITE *Milvus milvus* 73
A rare passage migrant and winter visitor.

This species has been recorded annually since 1985 with numbers increasing during the past decade. Most are recorded on spring passage (March to May), however, it has been noted in every month except June and November. Six were recorded during the national influx of spring 1988.

WHITE-TAILED EAGLE *Haliaeetus albicilla* 135
A very rare vagrant with 5 records, the last being in 1909.

MARSH HARRIER *Circus aeruginosus* 135
A rare passage migrant which has summered.

Numbers increasing with 8 records during the period. Most records are of immature birds in April-July and September. Surprisingly, the majority are from downland sites.

HEN HARRIER *Circus cyaneus* 135
A local winter visitor which has summered.

Numbers have remained constant with an average of five birds roosting each year during the period and at least ten birds present in total each winter. The birds are usually present from October to April on Salisbury Plain, downlands to the south-west of Salisbury and the Buttermere/Hippenscombe area. There have been several records of immatures summering.

MONTAGU'S HARRIER *Circus pygargus* 74
A scarce passage migrant which has bred.

Recorded less than annually though numbers are increasing. All records are between May and August in the south of the County.

GOSHAWK *Accipter gentilis* 136
A rare resident and vagrant with 18 records.

There have been at least 9 records during the period with most between February and April. Possibly up to 2 pairs have been present during the period but with no definite proof of breeding. Expanding populations nationally could lead to increases in the County.

SPARROWHAWK *Accipter nisus* 75
A common resident.

Numbers have fully recovered since the pesticide decline of the 1950's with the 22 breeding pairs reported in 1988 representing only a small proportion of the total population. This species has colonised urban areas with more success than any other raptor.

	1980	1981	1982	1983	1984	1985	1986	1987	1988	1989
Confirmed Breeding	4	9	9	16	17	15	15	16	22	22

BUZZARD *Buteo buteo* 75
A locally common resident, passage migrant and winter visitor.

There has been a dramatic rise in numbers over the past decade, due to both a real increase and better coverage. Most of the prime habitat in the south and west of the County is well populated, with densities in the north-east being the lowest, though even here breeding pairs have colonised new sites in the past few years.

Passage is noted annually, especially in October with birds moving south and west.

	1980	1981	1982	1983	1984	1985	1986	1987	1988	1989
Total Pairs Recorded	7	3	5	24	18	24	35	34	39	45

ROUGH-LEGGED BUZZARD *Buteo lagopus* 136
A rare winter visitor.

Most historic records were associated with national influxes, especially in 1975. There is, however, only one record during the period.

29 March to 11 April 1986: Imber - first winter bird.

OSPREY *Pandion haliaetus* 137
A scarce passage migrant which has summered.

An annual spring migrant with an April peak, fewer being recorded from August to September. Most records are from the Salisbury Avon and tributaries, lakes in the west of the County and the CWP. A bird summered at Shear Water in 1981. An average of 4 birds are recorded each year, with numbers increasing during the period, forty being recorded from 1980 to 1989, compared with twenty from 1956 to 1980.

KESTREL *Falco tinnunculus* 76
A common resident and passage migrant.

There has been no change in status during the period. Evidence of migration to and from the Continent for the winter has been supported by ringing recoveries.

Pullus 25.06.83 Bromham recovered 14.02.84 Calvados, France 253 kms
Pullus 22.07.85 Limburg, Holland recovered 04.11.85 Edington 565 kms

There is a successful nest box scheme underway on Salisbury Plain with 113 pulli being raised from 31 nests in 1989.

RED-FOOTED FALCON *Falco vespertinus* 137

An extremely rare spring migrant with 4 records, 2 of which were during the period and an additional record in 1990.

Since the first record in 1973 there has been a good sequence recently:

16-23 May 1988: CWP68 - immature male.
28-30 May 1989: CWP Swill Brook Bridge - immature pair.
27-29 May 1990: CWP68 - immature male.

MERLIN *Falco columbarius* 77
An uncommon winter visitor which has bred once prior to the period.

The most regular site, holding birds from September to April, is Salisbury Plain with up to seven birds present each winter. There has been a large increase in records away from traditional sites mainly due to better observer coverage; the species now being widely recorded from lowland areas, especially on passage.

HOBBY *Falco subbuteo* 77
An uncommon summer visitor.

There has been a steady increase in the number of breeding pairs, during the period, with birds occupying farmland and even suburbia, as well as more traditional woodland and downland sites. A pre-breeding gathering in May at CWP regularly reaches double figures.

	1980	1981	1982	1983	1984	1985	1986	1987	1988	1989
Number of sites	11	15	16	16	20	19	23	20	27	25
Pairs Proved Breeding	5	3	5	4	4	3	3	7	9	5
Pairs Probably Breeding	6	9	4	4	4	7	8	5	6	9
Pairs Possibly Breeding	0	3	7	8	12	10	15	9	14	12
Total Number of Pairs	11	15	16	16	20	20	26	21	29	26

GYR FALCON *Falco rusticolus* 137
An extremely rare vagrant with 2 records (1842 and 1906).

PEREGRINE *Falco peregrinus* 78
An uncommon winter visitor and passage migrant.

Annual records have increased by over fifty per cent during the period with birds regularly wintering in the County. All recent records, expect one, have been between August and April, with a November/January peak. Most spring and autumn records involve immatures, adults mostly appearing in early winter and leaving for breeding sites by the end of February. In the winter of 1988/89 birds roosted on Salisbury Cathedral, a site used for breeding in the 1930's. The most regular sites are CWP and the Salisbury area.

RED GROUSE *Lagopus lagopus* 138
An extremely rare vagrant (none since 1866).

BLACK GROUSE *Tetrao tetrix* 78
A former breeder (none since 1906).

RED-LEGGED PARTRIDGE *Alectoris rufa* 79
A locally common resident and introduced species.

Many coveys in the north-east of the County, where good numbers are put down for shooting, contain Chukar *Alectoris chukar* and the hybrid Ogridge.

GREY PARTRIDGE *Perdix perdix* 79
A common resident.

There has been a steady decline in numbers throughout the period reflecting the situation nationally. Agricultural changes affecting food for the chicks and reduced protection from predators for the nesting adults are thought to be significant contributory factors.

QUAIL *Coturnix coturnix* 79
A summer visitor in fluctuating numbers.

Records during the period were:

1980	1981	1982	1983	1984	1985	1986	1987	1988	1989
3	3	12	21	6	9	30	33	21	130

1989 numbers were unprecedented and reflected the situation nationally. Since 1986, the species has been covered by the Rare Breeding Birds Panel and details are as follows:

	1986	1987	1988	1989
Number of Sites	17	12	11	32
Pairs Proved Breeding	0	0	1	1
Pairs Probably Breeding	15	9	3	39
Pairs Possibly Breeding	15	24	17	90
Total Number of Pairs	30	33	21	130

Actual proof of breeding still remains frustratingly difficult.

PHEASANT *Phasianus colchicus* 80
A common resident whose numbers are maintained by introduction.

WATER RAIL *Rallus aquaticus* 138

R.H. Lye

A locally common winter visitor and extremely rare breeder.

Breeding first recorded at Coate Water in 1982 and Marlborough in 1987.

Possible origin of winter birds demonstrated by ringing recovery:

    Adult 16.04.82 Moen, Beligum, found dead Steeple Langford 21.02.85 375 kms.

SPOTTED CRAKE *Porzana porzana*   80
A rare vagrant which has bred (Mere 1881). Not recorded since 1971.

CORNCRAKE *Crex crex*   80
A very rare passage migrant which has bred but not since the 1950's. There were 7 records during the period, four of which were calling birds in spring. The remainder were autumn migrants, two of which were flushed by shoots at Bulford on 26 October 1985 and at Weather Hill Firs on 21 October 1989.

MOORHEN *Gallinula chloropus*   81
A common resident.

COOT *Fulica atra*   81
A common resident and winter visitor.

CRANE *Grus grus*   138
An extremely rare vagrant with 3 records, one of which was during the period and one additional record in 1990.

    1st and 2nd weeks of November 1988: Odstock Down, Salisbury - three.
    29 July 1990: Cholderton - one (the brief views did not entirely rule out other Crane species).

LITTLE BUSTARD *Tetrax tetrax*   138
An extremely rare vagrant with 3 records. Not recorded since 1952.

GREAT BUSTARD *Otis tarda*   81
A former resident with none this century.

The reintroduction scheme at Porton Down has now ceased as breeding attempts were unsuccessful.

OYSTERCATCHER *Haematopus ostralegus* 139
An uncommon passage migrant.

There has been a trend of increased records with 21 in 1988 alone. This species has been recorded in every month of the year with peaks in May and, more especially, July to September. The majority occur at CWP.

Number of birds per year and month:

1980	1981	1982	1983	1984	1985	1986	1987	1988	1989
0	4	5	3	9	11	9	15	21	5

Jan	Feb	Mar	Apr	May	June	July	Aug	Sept	Oct	Nov	Dec
0	3	7	2	9	3	17	25	9	3	3	1

BLACK-WINGED STILT *Himantopus himantopus* --
An extremely rare vagrant with 2 records (part of a national influx).

3-8 May 1987: Leckford Crossroads - one.
26 May 1987: CWP68 - a pair.

AVOCET *Recurvirostra avosetta* --

An extremely rare vagrant with 3 records.

19-23 July 1987: CWP68 - a pair.
1 May 1988: CWP Swill Brook - one.
16-24 June 1988: CWP68 - a pair.

STONE CURLEW *Burhinus oedicnemus* 82
A scare summer visitor.

Numbers of this species have remained at a fairly constant level during the period with the majority of pairs being on MOD Ranges. Most arrive in March and depart in October. Ringing recoveries suggest that passage is via south-west France, the adults wintering in southern Spain, whilst the first-winter birds reach North Africa. Wiltshire holds the record for the southern-most recovery of any Stone Curlew ringed in Europe.

Pullus June 1981 near Salisbury found dead Sierra Leone January 1982 4830 kms.

Post breeding moult flocks are occasionally discovered with a peak of thirty-one birds in 1986.

	1980	1981	1982	1983	1984	1985	1986	1987	1988	1989
Number of Sites	4	7	13	12	16	-	18	8	8	10
Pairs Proved Breeding	2	1	6	6	3	2	8	8	8	19
Pairs Probably Breeding	1	6	6	9	26	9	3	0	15	5
Pairs Possibly Breeding	1	0	1	5	6	19	7	0	0	1
Total Number of Pairs	4	7	13	20	35	30	18	8	23	25

CREAM-COLOURED COURSER *Cursorius cursor* 139
An extremely rare vagrant with 2 old records (1855 and 1896).

COLLARED PRATINCOLE *Glareola pratincola* 139
An extremely rare vagrant with 2 records (1852 and 1968).

LITTLE RINGED PLOVER *Charadrius dubius* 83
An uncommon summer visitor and passage migrant.

Numbers have increased over the past decade in relation to the availability of dry gravel pits. Records are mainly concentrated in CWP, the exception being two pairs which bred at Steeple Langford in 1980. The adults normally arrive in April and depart in July with juveniles lingering into September.

	1980	1981	1982	1983	1984	1985	1986	1987	1988	1989
CWP Total Pairs	2	5	2	2	2	1	2	10	10	8
Maximum Count Birds	-	-	-	-	11	7	9	42	32	27

Stone Curlew *Burhinus oedicnemus* B. Warren

RINGED PLOVER *Charadrius hiaticula*   139
An uncommon passage migrant and extremely rare breeder.

There has been a large increase in records from CWP with the peak passage in April-May and July-September; May being the best month. An unsuccessful breeding attempt occurred at CWP in 1989. The largest flock ever recorded was thirty in May 1988.

KENTISH PLOVER *Charadrius alexandrinus*   139

An extremely rare vagrant with 4 records, 2 of which were during the period.

5 May 1980: CWP26 - male.
3-4 May 1988: CWP68 - female.

DOTTEREL *Charadrius morinellus*   140
A very rare passage migrant with all recent records from high downland in spring.

1-3 May 1980: Hill Deverill - five.
28 May 1984: Casterley Camp - four.
6-12 May 1985: Hackpen - three.
9 May 1987: Edington - two.
22 April 1990: Stoford - two.

GOLDEN PLOVER *Pluvialis apricaria*   140
A locally common winter visitor and passage migrant.

There has been no change in status during the period with the major winter resorts being CWP, Marlborough Downs, the periphery of Salisbury Plain and the south-west corner of the County. Flocks reach 3000 at CWP and Wroughton, most occurring from November to February with a widespread passage in October and November. Hard weather causes desertion, birds often not returning again until the next winter.

GREY PLOVER *Pluvialis squatarola* 140
A scarce passage migrant.

With only 6 records prior to 1980 there have been over 30 during the period, and this species is now annual. All records are from September to May, with peaks in May and September/October. The number of records in November and December suggest some winter movement as well. The majority are from CWP.

Number of birds per year and month:

1980	1981	1982	1983	1984	1985	1986	1987	1988	1989
2	5	2	4	4	2	1	1	20	2

Jan	Feb	Mar	Apr	May	June	July	Aug	Sept	Oct	Nov	Dec
2	1	1	2	9	0	0	0	10	8	3	7

LAPWING *Vanellus vanellus* 84
A common resident and winter visitor.

This species has declined as a breeding bird due to changes in agricultural practices, with wet meadows and spring-sown cereals decreasing. The largest flocks occur from July to February with decreases in hard weather. Breeding sites are occupied by March. Several sites hold winter flocks exceeding 1000 birds: CWP, Broad Hinton, Zeals, Netheravon and Tytherington.

KNOT *Calidris canutus* 140
A rare passage migrant with 17 records, 10 of which were during the period.

This species occurs less than annually but is increasing. May and August-September are the peak months with most records from CWP.

SANDERLING *Calidris alba* 141
A rare passage migrant.

Records have increased since 1986, with all records during the period coming from CWP, May being the peak passage month. Most other records occurred from July to September. Twenty birds were recorded in 1987, including a flock of twelve on 17 May at CWP68.

Number of birds per year and month:

	1980	1981	1982	1983	1984	1985	1986	1987	1988	1989
	5	0	1	0	0	0	2	20	9	12

Jan	Feb	Mar	Apr	May	June	July	Aug	Sept	Oct	Nov	Dec
0	0	0	3	35	0	5	1	5	0	0	0

LITTLE STINT *Calidris minuta* 141
A scarce passage migrant.

Numbers have increased recently at CWP with records from every month except April, July and November. During the period there have been three spring birds, May to June, with the main passage occurring from August to October. One wintered from December 1988 to March 1989. The largest flock recorded was of fifteen birds on 3 September 1988 at CWP68.

Number of birds per year and month:

	1980	1981	1982	1983	1984	1985	1986	1987	1988	1989
	1	0	0	0	13	1	0	5	18	12

Jan	Feb	Mar	Apr	May	June	July	Aug	Sept	Oct	Nov	Dec
1	1	1	0	2	1	0	11	29	3	0	1

TEMMINCK'S STINT *Calidris temminckii* 31
A very rare vagrant with 9 records, 6 of which were during the period.

In contrast to the three September records of the 1970's, all recent sightings have been between 9 and 20 May.
  9-10 May 1987: CWP68 - two.
  17 May 1987: CWP Swill Brook - one.
  17 May 1988: CWP68 - one.
  18-20 May 1988: CWP68/73 - two.
  13 May 1989: CWP68 - one.

WHITE-RUMPED SANDPIPER *Calidris fuscicollis*
An extremely rare vagrant with only 1 record.

25-29 September 1988: CWP68 - an adult.

PECTORAL SANDPIPER *Calidris melanotos* 142
An extremely rare vagrant with 4 records, 3 of which were during the period, all involving single birds. Delete the October 1976 record from *The Birds of Wiltshire* which was incorrectly dated and referred to the October 1977 individual.

22-26 September 1984: CWP24.
17 May 1987: CWP Swill Brook.
25 September 1988: CWP68.

CURLEW SANDPIPER *Calidris ferruginea* 142
A rare passage migrant.

This species has become more regular during the period with most passage being from August to October, with two May records. 1988 was a record-breaking year for this species with a flock of 40 birds at CWP68 on 25 September.

Number of birds per year and month:

1980	1981	1982	1983	1984	1985	1986	1987	1988	1989
0	0	1	0	1	0	1	9	50	0

Jan	Feb	Mar	Apr	May	June	July	Aug	Sept	Oct	Nov	Dec
0	0	0	0	6	0	0	8	42	6	0	0

PURPLE SANDPIPER *Calidris maritima*   142
An extremely rare vagrant with only one old record (1881).

DUNLIN *Calidris alpina*   142
An uncommon passage migrant and winter visitor.

Numbers have increased during the period at CWP with peak passage occurring from April to May and July to October. A few now regularly winter at the CWP. Numbers depend on suitable dry pits being available. The largest flock recorded was of 28 in July 1988 at CWP68. There are very few records away from CWP.

BROAD-BILLED SANDPIPER *Limicola falcinellus*   142
An extremely rare vagrant with 2 records (1962 and 1977).

BUFF-BREASTED SANDPIPER *Tryngites subruficollis*   143
An extremely rare vagrant with only 1 record (1975).

RUFF *Philomachus pugnax*   143
An uncommon passage migrant and winter visitor.

T.M. Pinchen

Most records are from CWP with peak passage from April to May and August to September. Birds are regularly recorded in winter though not annually. The largest flock reported was of 42 in April 1987 at CWP68. Winter birds have often been recorded with Lapwing flocks in pasture and stubble fields.

JACK SNIPE *Lymnocryptes minimus* 143
An uncommon winter visitor.

This species is regularly recorded at Coate Water, CWP, Lacock GP, Rodbourne SF and Gare Hill. Numbers appear to remain constant although this is a difficult species to census. Most birds are present from October to March.

	1980	1981	1982	1983	1984	1985	1986	1987	1988	1989
CWP Maximum Count	0	0	4	4	7	5	1	4	3	5

SNIPE *Gallinago gallinago* 85
A common winter visitor and scarce summer visitor.

Numbers of breeding Snipe appear to have declined during the period due to land drainage, with none now breeding in the Thames Valley. Breeding now seems to be confined to the Salisbury Avon and the Kennet.

	1980	1981	1982	1983	1984	1985	1986	1987	1988	1989
Maximum Count (Drummers)	-	-	30	17	20	10	15	10	6	12

Wintering numbers remain constant at several sites, with the highest counts being at CWP, the Kennet, Salisbury Avon and Swindon SF though flocks exceeding 100 are becoming scarcer.

GREAT SNIPE *Gallinago media* 143
A very rare vagrant with 6 records, the last in 1936.

LONG-BILLED DOWITCHER *Limnodromus scolopaceus* 144
An extremely rare vagrant with only 1 record in 1974.

WOODCOCK *Scolopax rusticola* 85
An uncommon resident and winter visitor.

The number of sites occupied remains fairly constant, although the special survey in 1984 *(HOBBY 1985 p46)* produced a high count. This probably indicates a serious under-recording of the bird as a breeding species.

	1981	1982	1983	1984	1985	1986	1987	1988	1989
Number of Localities	10	7	8	61	13	11	16	11	12
Maximum Total (Roders)	-	-	-	159	-	26	41	21	32

BLACK-TAILED GODWIT *Limosa limosa* 144
A scarce passage migrant.

Numbers have increased with the species being recorded annually during the period. Peak passage is recorded from April to June and August to September, most records being from the CWP.

Number of birds per year and month:

1980	1981	1982	1983	1984	1985	1986	1987	1988	1989
0	1	6	5	11	3	7	2	20	20

Jan	Feb	Mar	Apr	May	June	July	Aug	Sept	Oct	Nov	Dec
0	0	3	4	6	11	4	28	19	0	0	0

BAR-TAILED GODWIT *Limosa lapponica* 144
A rare vagrant with 14 records, 6 of which were during the period and 2 additional records in 1990.

28 April 1986: Liden Lagoon - one.
20 December 1986: Boscombe Down - one.
22 December 1986: Rushall Down, Larkhill - one.
29 April to 15 May 1988: CWP68 - two (includes two records).
6-9 May 1989: CWP68 - one.
21 April 1990: CWP68 - two.
7 May 1990: CWP68 - two.

WHIMBREL *Numenius phaeopus* 144
An uncommon passage migrant.

There has been a marked increase in numbers over the period, April and May being the peak months, with fewer in July to August. The largest flock recorded was 13 in May 1988 at CWP Swill Brook.

CURLEW *Numenius arquata* 86
A scarce summer visitor and passage migrant which occasionally overwinters.

This wader is a summer visitor to the Thames and Bristol Avon, with the number of pairs increasing over the past decade. Birds are on their breeding sites from late February and depart in August/September. The post-breeding flock at CWP has been increasing with birds regularly wintering if the weather remains mild.

	1980	1981	1982	1983	1984	1985	1986	1987	1988	1989
Maximum Total (Pairs)	7	9	9	9	13	14	20	29	20	26
CWP Maximum Count	-	-	27	26	30	40	41	52	55	38

SPOTTED REDSHANK *Tringa erythropus* 145
A scarce passage migrant.

With over 25 records from 1947 up to and including 1979, there have been over 30 during the period with an annual average of 4 birds. It has been recorded in all months except December-February, with the main passage in April and August-September. Most records are from CWP.

Number of birds per year and month:

1980	1981	1982	1983	1984	1985	1986	1987	1988	1989
3	2	2	3	4	3	2	4	6	6

Jan	Feb	Mar	Apr	May	June	July	Aug	Sept	Oct	Nov	Dec
0	0	1	5	2	2	1	13	8	2	1	0

REDSHANK *Tringa totanus* 87
A scarce summer visitor and passage migrant.

Breeding numbers have declined during the period from up to 50 pairs in the late 1970's to an average of 20 pairs in the late 1980's. This has been mainly due to a loss of wet meadows.

Peak numbers occur in March and June, being scarce outside the breeding season. The Salisbury Avon and tributaries, Kennet and CWP are the main breeding sites.

Occasionally, single birds winter on flood meadows.

	1980	1981	1982	1983	1984	1985	1986	1987	1988	1989
Maximum Total (Pairs)	3	19	23	9	9	11	22	12	22	15

GREENSHANK *Tringa nebularia* 145
An uncommon passage migrant.

This wader has been recorded in every month (most records being from CWP) with peaks in May and July to September. Good spring passage is a fairly recent phenomenon, though August remains the best month. There has been the occasional winter record. The largest count was sixteen in August 1989 at CWP (various pits).

SOLITARY SANDPIPER *Tringa solitaria* 146
An extremely rare vagrant with only one record in 1966.

GREEN SANDPIPER *Tringa ochropus* 146
An uncommon passage migrant and winter visitor.

This species is present all year except for late May/early June. Passage is recorded in March, April and July-September, with a regular winter population from October to February. Declines are often recorded in January due to hard weather. A post breeding moult flock assembles at CWP from late June.

WOOD SANDPIPER *Tringa glareola* 146
A scarce passage migrant.

This species is recorded annually, May and August being the peak months with odd records for April, June, July and September. Numbers have remained constant throughout the decade, though with a slight increase since 1987. Most recent records are from CWP.

Number of birds per year and month:

1980	1981	1982	1983	1984	1985	1986	1987	1988	1989
0	1	2	3	2	1	2	3	4	4

Jan	Feb	Mar	Apr	May	June	July	Aug	Sept	Oct	Nov	Dec
0	0	0	1	7	2	1	10	1	0	0	0

COMMON SANDPIPER *Actitis hypoleucos* 87
An uncommon but regular passage migrant, rare winter visitor and extremely rare breeder.

A regular passage occurs in April-May and June-September with wintering occurring in five years of the past decade. No change in numbers has been noted. The species bred in 1980 at Steeple Langford GP.

TURNSTONE *Arenaria interpres* 146
A rare passage migrant.

Apart from an influx in 1988 (when a total of twelve birds occurred) the numbers of this species have remained constant, with an annual average of three recorded, May and August being the peak months. All records have been from CWP.

Number of birds per year and month:

1980	1981	1982	1983	1984	1985	1986	1987	1988	1989
3	0	3	1	2	0	0	3	12	2

Jan	Feb	Mar	Apr	May	June	July	Aug	Sept	Oct	Nov	Dec
0	0	0	1	12	0	4	16	4	0	0	0

RED-NECKED PHALAROPE *Phalaropus lobatus*   147
An extremely rare vagrant with 2 records (1841, 1990).

15 August 1990: Lacock GP - one.

GREY PHALAROPE *Phalaropus fulicarius*   147
A rare vagrant with 5 records during the period. These were all associated with autumn storms.

16 September 1983: Fonthill Lake - one.
4-14 October 1984: Coate Water - one.
4-8 October 1984: Tidworth SF - one.
16 October 1987: CWP68 - two.
17-18 September 1989: West Kennett - one.

POMARINE SKUA *Stercorarius pomarinus*   147
An extremely rare vagrant with 2 records, 1 of which was during the period.

11 November 1985: Swindon. One light phase adult in a party of seven Skuas in flight. The observer thought that the party probably consisted of six Pomarines and one Arctic but, due to the slight doubts involved, the record has been accepted as one Pomarine and six Skua species. There were records from many other inland counties during November 1985. This record occurred 100 years after the first, an immature at Sherston 1885.

ARCTIC SKUA *Stercorarius parasiticus*   147
A rare vagrant with 10 records, 3 of which were during the period.

19 October 1985: CWP, Ashton Keynes - dark phase.
10 November 1985: CWP68 - light phase adult.
9 September 1989: CWP68 - dark phase adult.

LONG-TAILED SKUA *Stercorarius longicaudus*   148
An extremely rare vagrant with one old record (1881).

GREAT SKUA *Stercorarius skua* 148
A very rare vagrant with 12 records, only one of which was during the period and one additional record in 1990. The first 10 records all occurred prior to 1885.

16 October 1987: White Sheet Hill. One in flight, obviously the result of the Great Storm.
4 February 1990: Southwick. One found exhausted which died the next day.

MEDITERRANEAN GULL *Larus melanocephalus* 148
An extremely rare vagrant with 4 records, 3 of which were during the period.

18 April 1982: Steeple Langford GP - adult in summer plumage.
2 April 1989: CWP32 - adult in summer plumage.
24/25/31 August and 1/2 September 1989: CWP68 - juvenile.

This last record possibly involved two birds as some plumage differences were noted by one observer.

LITTLE GULL *Larus minutus* 148
An uncommon passage migrant and winter visitor.

Of the 35 records during the period only 3 involved adults. Nineteen occurred at CWP; 10 at Coate Water; 3 at Steeple Langford GP; 2 at Liden Lagoon and 1 on the River Wylye at Great Wishford.

Number of birds per month:

Jan	Feb	Mar	Apr	May	June	July	Aug	Sept	Oct	Nov	Dec
0	0	1	4	2	0	1	9	10	3	2	3

SABINE'S GULL *Larus sabini* --
An extremely rare vagrant with only one record.
3 September 1983: CWP26 - an adult following severe westerly gales.

BLACK-HEADED GULL *Larus ridibundus* 148
A common winter visitor and passage migrant, summering in small numbers.

Pullus 15.06.83 Parnu, Estonia, recovered 11.08.83 Devizes 1817 kms
Pullus 17.06.81 Alyfus, Lithuania, recovered 24.10.83 Longleat 1776 km

These records indicate the origin of some of our passage birds.

RING-BILLED GULL *Larus delawarensis* --

An extremely rare vagrant with only one record.

1 April 1989: CWP68 - an adult.

COMMON GULL *Larus canus* 149
A common winter visitor and passage migrant.

LESSER BLACK-BACKED GULL *Larus fuscus* 149
A common passage migrant and winter visitor; also an extremely rare breeder.

Despite birds regularly summering and the close proximity of breeding colonies at Bath and Bristol, there has only been one confirmed breeding record at Trowbridge in 1986 on a factory roof.

HERRING GULL *Larus argentatus* 149
A regular but uncommon visitor, increasing.

Individuals of the yellow-legged races have been recorded in 1985 and annually since 1987.

ICELAND GULL *Larus glaucoides* 150
An extremely rare vagrant with only 1 record (1973).

47

GLAUCOUS GULL *Larus hyperboreus* --
An extremely rare vagrant with 4 records.

9-29 February 1984: CWP68 - a second winter bird. Probably the same individual seen again on 7 March. A "white" Gull at Swindon Tip on 22 February may have been this bird. However, there were substantial numbers of both Glaucous and Iceland Gulls in the south during 1984 and this bird could not be definitely assigned to one or other of these species.
30 December 1985: Swindon Tip - a first winter bird. An immature bird at the same place on 31 December showed features indicating hybrid origin, probably of Glaucous x Herring Gull parentage.
9 December 1987: Peatmoor Lagoon, Swindon - a second winter bird.
14 January 1990: CWP64 - a first winter bird.

GREAT BLACK-BACKED GULL *Larus marinus* 150
An uncommon but annual passage migrant and winter visitor.

KITTIWAKE *Rissa tridactyla* 150
An uncommon passage migrant and winter visitor. Number of birds per year and month:

1980	1981	1982	1983	1984	1985	1986	1987	1988	1989
0	0	1	17	3	3	4	0	29	7

Jan	Feb	Mar	Apr	May	June	July	Aug	Sept	Oct	Nov	Dec
2	2	3	5	3	0	0	2	1	1	1	0

The 1983 total includes a party of 12 at CWP in February and that of 1988, a party of 28 also at CWP in March.

IVORY GULL *Pagophila eburnea* 150
An extremely rare vagrant with only one record (1840).

CASPIAN TERN *Sterna caspia* --
An extremely rare vagrant with only one record.

15 August 1987: CWP68 - a first summer bird.

SANDWICH TERN *Sterna sandvicensis* 150
A scarce passage migrant, but increasing.

Number of birds per year:

1980	1981	1982	1983	1984	1985	1986	1987	1988	1989
9	1	5	0	10	0	1	6	7	2

There was only one spring record: an adult at CWP29 on 9 May 1989. Of the remainder, 2 were in July; 5 in August; 9 in September and one in October. Eleven records were from CWP; 3 from Coate Water; 2 from Steeple Langford GP; with singles at Shear Water and in flight over Swindon.

ROSEATE TERN *Sterna dougallii* 151
An extremely rare vagrant with 2 records, 1 of which was during the period.

11 May 1989: CWP29 - an adult in summer plumage.

COMMON TERN *Sterna hirundo* 87
A regular passage migrant and very rare breeder.

After initial success at CWP in 1979 and 1980 a gap of five years followed before breeding was attempted again in 1986. Since then one or two pairs have nested annually at the CWP but do not always succeed beyond the egg or small young stages.

ARCTIC TERN *Sterna paradisaea* 151
An uncommon but regular passage migrant.

Number of birds per year and month:

1980	1981	1982	1983	1984	1985	1986	1987	1988	1989
3	0	4	2	2	2	4	14	18	17

Jan	Feb	Mar	Apr	May	June	July	Aug	Sept	Oct	Nov	Dec
0	0	0	2	11	1	0	6	9	3	0	0

The majority of records come from the CWP and Coate Water, the only other sites being Shear Water and Steeple Langford GP.

LITTLE TERN *Sterna albifrons* 151
Rare passage migrant with 19 records, 12 of which were during the period.

Number of birds per year and month:

1980	1981	1982	1983	1984	1985	1986	1987	1988	1989
0	1	2	3	1	0	0	4	0	8

Jan	Feb	Mar	Apr	May	June	July	Aug	Sept	Oct	Nov	Dec
0	0	0	1	3	0	1	4	3	0	0	0

All the April, May and July records occurred in one year, 1989.

BLACK TERN *Chlidonias niger* 151
A regular but uncommon passage migrant.

The species is recorded less often in spring than autumn. Spring records have occurred at more varied localities, those in autumn tend to be concentrated at CWP, Coate Water and to a lesser extent Steeple Langford GP. Autumn passage was particularly heavy in 1980, '82 and '89; the largest single flocks being at the CWP: 40 in September 1980 and 35 in August 1989. A bird remained on the River Avon, Melksham from 8-22 November 1984, a remarkably late date.

WHITE-WINGED BLACK TERN *Chlidonias leucopterus* --

An extemely rare vagrant with only one record.

24-29 September 1982: CWP26 - an immature.

GUILLEMOT *Uria aalge* 152
An extremely rare vagrant with 3 records; none since 1916.

RAZORBILL *Alca torda* 152
An extremely rare vagrant with 3 records; none this century.

LITTLE AUK *Alle alle* 152
A rare vagrant with 19 records, 2 of which were during the period and an additional 2 records in 1990.

10 January 1984: Malmesbury.
17 January 1984: Coate Water. Picked up exhausted and died same day.
29 December 1990: Tisbury - one, released on the coast.
29 December 1990: Shalbourne - one, died following day.

PUFFIN *Fratercula arctica* 152
A rare vagrant with 18 records, 2 of which were during the period.

12 September 1983: Corsham - one grounded, later released.
5 March 1988: Devizes - an adult found dead on dual carriageway.

PALLAS'S SANDGROUSE *Syrrhaptes paradoxus* 152
An extremely rare vagrant with 2 records; none this century.

STOCK DOVE *Columba oenas* 88
A common resident.

WOOD PIGEON *Columba palumbus* 88
A very common resident.

COLLARED DOVE *Streptopelia decaocto* 88
A common resident.

TURTLE DOVE *Streptopelia turtur* 89
A summer visitor.

There has been a continued decline throughout the period corresponding with National CBC results.

CUCKOO *Cuculus canorus* 89
A common summer visitor.

Despite conflicting reports, throughout the period numbers appear to have remained stable.

BARN OWL *Tyto alba* 90
An uncommon resident.

After the steady decline of the 1960's which continued into the early 1980's, there has been a definite increase in numbers. A substantial effort in the provision of nest boxes has, undoutedly, benefitted this species. Seventeen of the 34 pairs breeding in 1989 used these boxes. Breeding pairs:

1980	1981	1982	1983	1984	1985	1986	1987	1988	1989
3	3	3	9	20	12	21	16	22	34

SCOPS OWL *Otus scops* 153
An extremely rare vagrant with 4 records, one of which was during the period.

6/7 June 1982: Upton Scudamore - one calling.
13/14 July 1982: Warminster, School of Infantry.

The appearance at Upton Scudamore, a short distance from Warminster was probably an isolated foray as the bird had apparently been present at the School of Infantry since April, the first for 109 years.

SNOWY OWL *Nyctea scandiaca* 153
An extremely rare vagrant with only one record (1945).

HAWK OWL *Surnia ulula* 153
An extremely rare vagrant with only one old record (1850).

LITTLE OWL *Athene noctua* 90
A common resident.

TAWNY OWL *Strix aluco* 90
A common resident.

LONG-EARED OWL *Asio otus* 91
A very rare resident and scarce winter visitor.

	1980	1981	1982	1983	1984	1985	1986	1987	1988	1989
Breeding Pairs	1	0	0	0	3	0	0	2	2	0
Number of Birds During Winter Period	5	4	5	4	13	8	4	8	10	4

SHORT-EARED OWL *Asio flammeus* 91
A regular winter visitor and extremely rare breeder.

There have been no summering birds or evidence of breeding during the period. Winter numbers fluctuate considerably. The species is rarely recorded away from MOD land or the Marlborough Downs.

NIGHTJAR *Caprimulgus europaeus* 91
A rare, local and decreasing summer visitor.

The species has continued to decline and is now virtually confined to Grovely Wood, Longleat and the woodlands south and east of Salisbury. The former sites of Southleigh and Eastleigh Wood have been unoccupied since 1985. For some reason, however, there was a marked increase in 1989.

	1980	1981	1982	1983	1984	1985	1986	1987	1988	1989
Number of Pairs	7	11	3	13	8	11	9	4	6	13
Number of Sites	5	7	1	7	5	4	7	2	2	6

SWIFT *Apus apus* 92
A common summer visitor.

ALPINE SWIFT *Apus melba* 153
An extremely rare vagrant with 3 records, 2 of which were during the period.

12/13 July 1984: Swindon.
29 June 1986: Morgan's Hill.

KINGFISHER *Alcedo atthis* 92
A common resident.

With the recent series of mild winters, numbers remain high.

BEE-EATER *Merops apiaster* 153
An extremely rare vagrant with only one old record (1866).

ROLLER *Coracias garrulus* 153
An extremely rare vagrant with 2 records (1883, 1947).

HOOPOE *Upupa epops* 93
A rare passage migrant and very rare breeder.

Of the 17 records during the period, 13 have been of birds on spring passage, 9 of these occurring in April. Of the others, one was in July, 2 in October and the most unusual an individual at CWP from 4-8 December 1982. There has been no evidence of breeding since 1971.

Nightjar *Caprimulgus europaeus* D.R. Kjaer

WRYNECK *Jynx torquilla* 93
A rare autumn passage migrant and former breeder.

All but one have occurred between 26 August and 7 October, the majority being in September. The species did not occur during 1980-83 or 1988, the largest number being 7 in 1984, coinciding with an above average influx into the country during that period. One in song in the north of the County on 10 June 1986 was presumably a migrant, the species not having bred in the County since 1950.

One ringed 05.09.89 Icklesham, Sussex, recovered 11.09.89 Marlborough 176 kms

GREEN WOODPECKER *Picus viridis* 93
A common resident.

Less frequently encountered in the north-east of the County.

GREAT SPOTTED WOODPECKER *Dendrocopos major* 94
A common resident.

The increase of the late 1970's has levelled out and there has been a slight decrease in some areas during the last five years.

A bird ringed at Queen Mary Reservoir, Surrey was found dead on 2 May 1987 at Bradford-on-Avon (123 kms). Movements of more than 100 kms are very unusual and most have been associated with autumn arrivals along the east coast.

LESSER SPOTTED WOODPECKER *Dendrocopos minor* 95
An uncommon and local resident.

This species still remains an elusive one. Annual records average 9 breeding pairs, with the number of sites at which the species is recorded ranging from 16 to 28.

WOODLARK *Lullula arborea* 95
A very rare winter visitor and extremely rare breeder.

Since 1963 there have been no confirmed breeding records but 2 pairs were present in suitable habitat during 1986, 1988 and 1989 and the species probably bred in those years. The only other records were 3 birds seen near Landford on 20 November and 4 December 1983 and also at Landford in February and November 1984.

SKYLARK *Alauda arvensis* 95
A common resident, passage migrant and winter visitor.

Great Spotted Woodpecker *Dendrocopos major*   *D.R. Kjaer*

SAND MARTIN *Riparia riparia* 96
An uncommon passage migrant and summer visitor.

After the decrease in the late 1970's due to the Sahel drought, the species crashed again in 1984 and 1985 with numbers at their lowest ever. From 1986, however, there has been a marked recovery and an annual increase. There are only three regular colonies; at Calne, CWP and Salisbury, the colony at Westbury not surviving after 1984.

SWALLOW *Hirundo rustica* 96
A common summer visitor.

Records indicate a very slight decline over the period.

HOUSE MARTIN *Delichon urbica* 97
A common summer visitor.

Numbers have remained stable although fluctuations have been noted in different areas.

RICHARD'S PIPIT *Anthus novaeseelandiae* --
An extremely rare vagrant with only one record.

16 September 1986: Ebsbury Hill, Wishford - one.

TAWNY PIPIT *Anthus campestris* --
An extremely rare vagrant with only one record.

27-29 September 1983: Colerne Airfield - a juvenile.

TREE PIPIT *Anthus trivialis* 97
A common but local summer visitor.

The slight downward trend in National CBC results has been reflected in Wiltshire, where the species is now quite local and rarely recorded away from traditional sites even on passage.

MEADOW PIPIT *Anthus pratensis* 97
A common breeder, winter visitor and passage migrant.

Passage occurs during March/April and on a larger scale during September/October. 1986 passage was particularly heavy with 1000 at Larkhill and 500 at Imber.

ROCK PIPIT *Anthus petrosus* 153
An extremely rare vagrant with 6 records, 2 of which were during the period and two additional records in 1990.

1 January 1982: Eysey, Cricklade - one.
17 October 1988: CWP68 - one.
8 April 1990: CWP68 - one.
29 Sept 1990: CWP68 - one.

WATER PIPIT *Anthus spinoletta* 153
A rare passage migrant and winter visitor.

The species averages 2 records annually with 1988 being the only blank year. Britford and CWP have been the most favoured sites.

YELLOW WAGTAIL *Motacilla flava* 98
A common passage migrant, breeding in small numbers.

The number of breeding pairs has decreased considerably in recent years. Individuals showing characteristics of the race *Motacilla f. flava* have been recorded at Coate Water during April in every year except 1987, whilst in 1980 a male stayed there from the end of April until mid-June. The only other site to record this race was Rodbourne SF in July and August 1985. A male showing the characteristics of the race *Motacilla f. thunbergi* was seen at Coate Water in July 1983.

GREY WAGTAIL *Motacilla cinerea* 98
A common resident.

There has been evidence of a marked autumn passage together with an increase in numbers during winter in several years.

PIED WAGTAIL *Motacilla alba* 99
A common resident, passage migrant and winter visitor.

Winter numbers are increased by birds moving down from the north of the country. Ringing recoveries supporting this were:

    Adult 31.12.78 Bratton, recovered 20.05.81 Beddgelert, Gwynedd 235 kms
    Juvenile 31.08.84 Morpeth, recovered 16.10.84 Swindon 400 kms

Larger roosts have occurred at CWP; Devizes Market Place; Roussel Factory, Swindon; Swindon Police HQ; Trowbridge Tescos and Warminster Safeways.

Birds of the nominate race (White Wagtail) are regular passage migrants in small numbers particularly in spring.

WAXWING *Bombycilla garrulus* 154
A rare winter visitor with 6 records during the period.

T.M. Pinchen

23 March 1985: Calne - two.
3 January 1987: Nythe, Swindon - one with two there on 20 March.
21 December 1988: Imber Village - one.
18 January 1989: West Swindon - two in flight.
29 January 1989: Box - one.
28 February 1989: Downton - one.

DIPPER *Cinclus cinclus*   100
A rare local resident.

Strongholds are still the ByBrook (Box-Castle Combe); Wylye (south of Warminster) and the Frome (at Tellisford). Probably no more than 15 pairs breed annually.

WREN *Troglodytes troglodytes*   100
A common resident.

DUNNOCK *Prunella modularis*   100
A common resident.

ROBIN *Erithacus rubecula*   101
A common resident.

NIGHTINGALE *Luscinia megarhynchos*   101
An uncommon summer visitor.

The 1980 survey of this species produced a total of 195 singing males, an increase of 23 over that of the 1976 survey. Numbers have probably decreased slightly in recent years as habitat changes occur.

BLUETHROAT *Luscinia svecica*   154
An extremely rare vagrant with 3 records; none since 1972.

BLACK REDSTART *Phoenicurus ochruros*   101
An uncommon passage migrant, winter visitor and very rare breeder.

There have been 5 confirmed breeding records but none since 1979, although singing males were present during the breeding season in 1981, 1982 and 1988.

The species has appeared in every month of the year although April-May and October-December are the periods of commonest occurrence. Worthy of note is the influx in November and December 1982 involving 16 individuals.

REDSTART *Phoenicurus phoenicurus* 102
An uncommon summer visitor and passage migrant.

There has been a slight increase over the last 10 years but the annual total of breeding pairs has never exceeded 30.

WHINCHAT *Saxicola rubetra* 102
A locally common summer visitor and uncommon passage migrant.

Confined mainly to the MOD Range areas, a survey of these areas by the Conservation Groups in 1987 produced a total of 111 pairs. A number of these pairs were found on land over which access had previously been much restricted, so it is probable that this vast increase over the 50 pairs published in *The Birds of Wiltshire* is due to increased coverage and not a population expansion.

STONECHAT *Saxicola torquata* 103
A scarce resident, winter visitor and passage migrant.

The species breeds regularly on the MOD Ranges and since 1987 at Pound Bottom. It has also reared young during the period at Aldbourne; Old Sarum and Pepperbox Hill. The hard weather of early 1982 hit the breeding population and the species has still not fully recovered. A few migrants are seen regularly in suitable habitat and wintering birds swell the numbers in the regular breeding areas from October to March.

	1980	1981	1982	1983	1984	1985	1986	1987	1988	1989
Number of Breeding Pairs	15	12	4	8	8	10	6	12	7	10

From 21 November 1987 to 7 February 1988: a female of one of the Eastern races *(S.t.maura or stejnegeri),* known as the Siberian Stonechat, was present at Chirton Gorse, Larkhill - the first County record.

WHEATEAR *Oenanthe oenanthe* 103
A common passage migrant and extremely rare breeder.

There have only been 3 confirmed breeding records during the period: at Larkhill in 1986; Porton Down in 1988 and Wylye Down 1989. Passage is prolonged and in some years, heavy, a count of 86 at Larkhill on 29 March 1987 being noteworthy.

RING OUZEL *Turdus torquatus* 154
An uncommon passage migrant.

Of the 35 records during the period, only 2 have been in autumn, both during October. From 1980 to 1986 only 7 birds were recorded on spring passage, so that of April 1987, involving 14 individuals, was most unexpected.

BLACKBIRD *Turdus merula* 104
A common resident whose winter numbers are augmented by birds from the Continent.

Ringing recoveries supporting this are:

  Adult 10.02.80 Corsham, recovered 06.04.81 Turku-Pori, Finland 1787 kms
  Adult 15.12.84 Edington, recovered 27.03.89 Nidingen on Sala, Sweden 1124 kms
  One 04.11.89 Falsterbo, Sweden recovered 08.12.89 Edington 1088 kms
  One 20.11.88 Sells Green recovered 09.08.90 Gatehouse of Fleet, Dumfries and Galloway 417 kms

FIELDFARE *Turdus pilaris* 155
A common winter visitor.

SONG THRUSH *Turdus philomelos* 104
A common resident.

With the recent spate of dry summers causing difficulties in the feeding of nestlings, breeding success has been poor and numbers have declined considerably.

REDWING *Turdus iliacus* 155
A common winter visitor.

MISTLE THRUSH *Turdus viscivorus*   105
A common resident.

Post breeding flocks of between 30-50 birds, consisting mainly of juveniles, occur annually with the largest record at Corsham, 62 on 28.09.89.

CETTI'S WARBLER *Cettia cetti*   --
A rare resident increasing in numbers.

First recorded in the County on 30 October 1980 at Coate Water and subsequently on 3 October 1981 at Coate Water; 12 August 1985 at Steeple Langford and 13 October 1985 at Britford.

First breeding record from Petersfinger in 1987 where it probably bred in both 1988 and 1989; also present at Standlynch in 1987, 1988 and 1989 and may have bred.

A significant increase in records of singing males in 1990, mainly in river valleys to the south of Salisbury following a succession of mild winters.

GRASSHOPPER WARBLER *Locustella naevia*   105
An uncommon summer visitor which breeds locally.

SAVI'S WARBLER *Locustella luscinioides*   155
An extremely rare vagrant with only one record in May 1965.

AQUATIC WARBLER *Acrocephalus paludicola*   156
An extremely rare vagrant with 3 records in 1958, 1970 and 1972.

SEDGE WARBLER *Acrocephalus schoenobaenus*   105
A common summer visitor which breeds mainly in damp areas.

MARSH WARBLER *Acrocephalus palustris*   106
A formerly scarce summer visitor which bred in 1980 and 1983.

Only one further record of a bird in song at CWP (Waterhay Bridge) on 27 June 1987. As the individual was not relocated the record probably relates to a passage bird.

REED WARBLER *Acrocephalus scirpaceus*   106
A common summer visitor which breeds wherever there are sufficient Phragmites.

Juvenile 06.09.81 Corsham Lake, recovered 13.08.84 Casablanca, Morocco 2024 kms

Reed Warbler *Acrocephalus scirpaceus*   *D.R. Kjaer*

ICTERINE WARBLER *Hippolais icterina*   156
An extremely rare vagrant with 2 records.

A pair was reputed to have bred in 1907 (not 1970 as stated in *The Birds of Wiltshire*) and a singleton was recorded in 1944.

MELODIOUS WARBLER *Hippolais polyglotta*   156
An extremely rare vagrant with only one record in 1966.

DARTFORD WARBLER *Sylvia undata*   107
A former resident which was only recorded at one site sporadically in 1988, the first record since 1976. Bred on County boundary in 1990.

BARRED WARBLER *Sylvia nisoria*   --

An extremely rare vagrant with only one record.

6 September 1980: Coate Water - an immature.

LESSER WHITETHROAT *Sylvia curruca*   107
A common summer visitor.

One 01.09.87 Bromham recovered Alexandropolis, Greece 17.10.87 2439 kms

WHITETHROAT *Sylvia communis*   108
A common summer visitor.

Scarcer in the early years of the period. The population has recovered significantly since the late 1970's.

GARDEN WARBLER *Sylvia borin*   108
A common summer visitor.

Two ringing records of interest:
    One 08.06.80 Clanger Wood retrapped same location July 1987
    One 30.05.83 Clanger Wood retrapped same location June 1990.
Both birds older than the oldest known British ringed bird *(Ringing & Migration Dec 1990)*.

BLACKCAP *Sylvia atricapilla* 108
A common summer and uncommon, but widespread, winter visitor.

Two ringing records of interest:

> One 30.04.87 Great Wood, Grittenham recovered 25.03.90 Ighzer Amokrane, Algeria 1745 kms
> Adult 30.04.88 Edington, recovered 30.12.89 Mechtras Tizi-Ouzou, Algeria 1711 kms

YELLOW-BROWED WARBLER *Phylloscopus inornatus* 156
A very rare vagrant with 7 records, 6 of which were during the period.

4 October 1986: Melksham - one.
17 October 1986: Hankerton - one.
3/4 November 1986: Lydiard Park - one.
6 October 1987: The Lawn, Swindon - one.
8 November 1987: CWP68 - one.
24-29 September 1988: Coate Water - one.

WOOD WARBLER *Phylloscopus sibilatrix* 109
A summer visitor which breeds locally.

Its stronghold is the woodland bordering the New Forest.

CHIFFCHAFF *Phylloscopus collybita* 109
A common summer and uncommon winter visitor favouring damp places.

Two winter records in 1987 and 1989 showed characteristics of the Scandinavian race, *P.c.abietinus*.

One ringing record of interest:

> One 30.07.87 Great Wood, Grittenham, recovered 18.11.87 Parc National du Djoudj, Senegal 4081 kms.

WILLOW WARBLER *Phylloscopus trochilus* 110
A common summer visitor.

GOLDCREST *Regulus regulus* 110
A common resident, winter visitor and passage migrant.

Some CBC results indicated a dramatic decline in breeding numbers following the hard winter weather in mid-period. The subsequent mild winters have allowed a steady increase in the breeding population.

Two interesting ringing recoveries:
One 28.09.83 Isle of May, Fife, recovered 11.03.84 Bromham 534 kms
One 26.10.85 St Margaret's, Kent, recovered 09.11.85 Dilton Marsh 250 kms

FIRECREST *Regulus ignicapillus* 156
An extremely rare breeder, scarce winter visitor and passage migrant.

	1980	1981	1982	1983	1984	1985	1986	1987	1988	1989
Number of Sites	-	-	-	1	2	2	0	3	2	2
Pairs Proved Breeding	-	-	-	1	0	0	0	0	0	0
Pairs Probably Breeding	-	-	-	0	0	2	0	4	2	2
Pairs Possibly Breeding	-	-	-	0	3	0	0	2	1	1
Total Number of Pairs	-	-	-	1	3	2	0	6	3	3

SPOTTED FLYCATCHER *Muscicapa striata* 110
A common summer visitor.

One interesting ringing recovery:

Pullus 21.06.87 Longbridge Deverill, recovered 07.10.87 Ndobo Village, Ukwonyo, Ytonkon, Nigeria 5004 kms in 108 days.

RED-BREASTED FLYCATCHER *Ficedula parva* 157
An extremely rare vagrant with only one record in May 1944.

PIED FLYCATCHER *Ficedula hypoleuca* 157
An extremely rare breeder and regular passage migrant in small numbers.

More spring than autumn records during the period with an exceptional 25 birds in spring 1985.

First confirmed breeding in 1986 from Longleat. On five occasions during the period (1984, 1985, 1987, 1988 and 1989) males were located singing in suitable breeding habitat, once with a female present, but in all cases breeding was not proven.

One ringing recovery of interest:

Adult 10.04.85 Bratton controlled at nestbox 10.06.85 Llanfair, Clwyd 239 kms.

BEARDED TIT *Panurus biarmicus* 157
A rare vagrant with 15 records, one of which was during the period.

16 October 1982: Coate Water - a male and female.

LONG-TAILED TIT *Aegithalos caudatus* 111
A common resident.

Wiltshire ringing records have shown this bird to be particularly long lived with six records of bird surviving five years or more, and one bird still going strong after seven years:

Juvenile 01.07.82 Clanger Wood retrapped same location 01.04.90.

The above bird was caught thirteen times between first and last capture!

MARSH TIT *Parus palustris* 111
A common resident.

WILLOW TIT *Parus montanus* 111
An uncommon, local resident which is more frequently reported from high ground than the Marsh Tit.

COAL TIT *Parus ater* 112
A common resident.

BLUE TIT *Parus caeruleus* 112
A common resident.

GREAT TIT *Parus major* 112
A common resident.

NUTHATCH *Sitta europaea* 112
A locally common resident.

TREECREEPER *Certhia familiaris* 113
A common resident.

H.G. Phelps

GOLDEN ORIOLE *Oriolus oriolus* 157
A scarce visitor with one record during the period.

Late May 1981: Pewsey Manor - a pair.

RED-BACKED SHRIKE *Lanius collurio* 113
An extremely rare visitor which was formerly a common breeder.

Two records in the period:

31 August 1980: Between Biddestone and Slaughterford - a male.
25 July 1983: Westbury - a female.

LESSER GREY SHRIKE *Lanius minor* 158
An extremely rare vagrant with only one record (June 1965).

GREAT GREY SHRIKE *Lanius excubitor* 158
A scarce winter visitor recorded in nine out of ten years of the period.

WOODCHAT SHRIKE *Lanius senator* 158
A very rare vagrant with 5 records, the last in 1974.

JAY *Garrulus glandarius* 114
A common resident.

An exceptional westerly migration in Autumn 1983 was part of a nationally noted movement.

MAGPIE *Pica pica* 114
A common resident.

NUTCRACKER *Nucifraga caryocatactes* 158
An extremely rare vagrant with 4 records, all from 1968-1969.

CHOUGH *Pyrrhocorax pyrrhocorax* 158
A very rare vagrant with 5 old records (none this century).

JACKDAW *Corvus monedula* 114
A common resident.

ROOK *Corvus frugilegus* 114
A common resident.

Very little recent data is available on the changes in number and size of rookeries in the County, but see *HOBBY 1981 p.33, A Sample Census of Rookeries 1980*.

CARRION CROW *Corvus corone corone* 115
A common resident and winter visitor.

Only one record of the race *C.c.cornix* (Hooded Crow) during the period at Swindon on 18 November 1983.

RAVEN *Corvus corax* 115
A scarce visitor which formerly bred, with 3 records during the period.

6 November 1982: near County boundary at Cerney Wick.
Mid-October to end November 1983: Steeple Ashton/Keevil area.
3 December 1983: Probably same individual as Steeple Ashton/Keevil.
8 August 1984: Upper Westwood.

STARLING *Sturnus vulgaris* 115
A common resident and winter visitor.

One 19.01.87 Chippenham recovered 03.06.87 Sodermanland, Sweden 1447 kms.

An example of the origin of some of the wintering birds.

ROSE-COLOURED STARLING *Sturnus roseus* 159
A very rare vagrant with 7 records, the last in July 1972.

HOUSE SPARROW *Passer domesticus* 115
A common resident.

TREE SPARROW *Passer montanus*   116
An uncommon, local resident mainly recorded in the north of the County. Less common than formerly.

CHAFFINCH *Fringilla coelebs*   116
A common resident and winter visitor.

Two ringing recoveries show the origin of some of the wintering birds:

> Adult 12.03.83 Bratton, recovered 25.08.85 Orboholm Trosa, Sodermanland, Sweden 1500 kms
> Adult 19.11.83 Westbury recovered 03.08.85 Grimstadvatnet, Hareid, Norway 1330 kms.

BRAMBLING *Fringilla montifringilla*   159
An irregular winter visitor.

Largest reported flocks in the period were c250 at The Stonehenge Inn on 27 February 1981 and 250 at Barford on 2 January 1982.

GREENFINCH *Carduelis chloris*   116
A common resident and winter visitor.

Well represented in ringing reports in *HOBBY*, in particular see *Partial Migration of Greenfinch to and from Chippenham, HOBBY 1983 p.42*.

GOLDFINCH *Carduelis carduelis*   116
A common resident and passage migrant.

One interesting ringing recovery:

> Juvenile 14.08.83 East Tytherton, recovered 29.12.83 Sidi Kacem, Morocco 1939 kms.

SISKIN *Carduelis spinus*   159
An extremely rare breeder and common winter visitor.

First breeding record in 1987; also bred in 1988 and 1989.

> One 13.03.88 Shear Water, recovered 05.10.88 Beek, Limburg, The Netherlands 561 kms
> Adult 06.04.88 Shear Water recovered 29.03.89 Staouali, Algeria 1652 kms later recovered February 1990 at Flackwell Heath, Buckinghamshire.

LINNET *Carduelis cannabina*   117
A common resident and passage migrant.

Tree Sparrow *Passer montanus*   H.G. Phelps

Brambling *Fringilla montifringilla*   D.R. Kjaer

Goldfinch *Carduelis carduelis*   *D.R. Kjaer*

Siskin *Carduelis spinus*   *D.R. Kjaer*

TWITE *Carduelis flavirostris* 160
A very rare vagrant with 6 records, 2 of which were during the period and an additional record in 1990.
22 February 1983: Shear Water - three.
18 October 1989: Codford - two.
7 November 1990: Shear Water - one.

REDPOLL *Carduelis flammea* 117
An irregular breeder and common winter visitor.

The largest flock recorded in the period was 150 at Shear Water on 19 January 1983. The only regular breeding area is now in the south-east of the County.

A bird showing the characteristics of the race *C.f.flammea* (Mealy Redpoll) seen at Picket Wood on 20 February 1982 and a very pale individual, possibly of this race, at CWP26 on 22 February 1987.

One 06.04.88 Shear Water recovered 14.05.88 Selby, North Yorkshire was probably in its breeding territory; see *HOBBY 1989 p.76, Redpoll and Siskin Weights and Migration.*

CROSSBILL *Loxia curvirostra* 118
An uncommon local resident and irruptive passage migrant.

D.R. Kjaer

The largest flocks reported in the period were: up to 50 during October/November 1982 in the Shearwater-Longleat area and 50 at Penstones Wood on 24 February 1984.

BULLFINCH *Pyrrhula pyrrhula*   118
A common resident.

HAWFINCH *Coccothraustes coccothraustes*   118
An uncommon resident and irruptive migrant.

The largest number recorded during the period was up to 15 at Savernake Forest from 1 January to 12 March 1989, and the species was widespread at this time following a national influx.

LAPLAND BUNTING *Calcarius lapponicus*   160
An extremely rare vagrant with only one record in December 1953.

SNOW BUNTING *Plectrophenax nivalis*   160
A rare vagrant with 6 records during the period and one additional record in 1990.

11 December 1983: Roundway Hill - one male.
14 March 1987: CWP38 and presumably the same bird at CWP26 on 28 March 1987 - one female.
7 February 1988: CWP37 - one male.
29 November 1989: Tollard Royal - one.
30 November 1989: Boscombe Down - one.
4-9 December 1989: Bratton - one.
2 December 1990: Morgan's Hill - one.

YELLOWHAMMER *Emberiza citrinella*   118
A common resident.

CIRL BUNTING *Emberiza cirlus*   119
A former breeder, now extremely rare vagrant with 2 records during the period.

January/February 1980: Winterslow - one.
18 October 1980: Low Lane Pits, Calne - an immature male.

These records reflect the national decline and contraction in range of this species.

ORTOLAN BUNTING *Emberiza hortulana* --
An extremely rare vagrant with only one record.

I.W. Grier

26 September 1986: Thorncombe, Bratton - first year bird; ringed.

LITTLE BUNTING *Emberiza pusilla* --
An extremely rare vagrant with only one record.

27 March 1989: Bromham - first year female; ringed.

REED BUNTING *Emberiza schoeniclus* 119
A common resident and winter visitor.

A ringing recovery of interest may point to the origin of some winter birds:
One 15.06.84 Gronant, Clwyd, recovered 27.12.84 Corsham 235 kms

CORN BUNTING *Miliaria calandra* 120
A locally common resident.
The largest flock reported during the period was 342 at Westdown (Salisbury Plain) on 16 December 1982.

ESCAPES (1980 - 1989 INCLUSIVE)

By S.B. Edwards, S.M. Palmer and R. Turner.

In every County avifaunal list the thorny problem arises of the escape from captive collections, deliberate releases of non-resident species, etc. Wiltshire is no exception to this and over the years obvious escapes such as Budgerigar and Canary through to the less obvious escapes such as Pink-footed Goose and Ruddy Shelduck have taxed the County Records Panel's brains.

Where there has been suspicion as to the origin of a bird, this has been reported in the Systematic List of this publication and the appropriate year's *HOBBY*. If there is no doubt that the bird is an escape it has simply been listed as such after the Systematic List in each year's *HOBBY*. Records of some species include both escapes and genuine wild birds. Where this is the case, cross reference is made between this chapter and the Systematic List.

In view of the confusion and uncertainty created by this particular group of birds, it has been decided that only the species name and the year of recording will be included. If further data is required, reference should be made to the appropriate copy of *HOBBY*.

The list below is not in Voous order and the year referred to is the year the birds were sighted, not the year of *HOBBY*. The obvious cagebird escapes have been omitted.

Species	Year/s Sighted
Sacred Ibis *Threskiornis aethiopica*	1981, 1983
Black Swan *Cygnus atratus*	1981, 1984-86, 1988, 1989
Bean Goose *Anser fabalis*	1983
Pink-footed Goose *Anser brachyrhynchus*	1982, 1983, 1986-88 (see Systematic List)
Lesser White-fronted Goose *Anser erythropus*	1986, 1987
Snow Goose *Anser caerulescens*	1981-88
Barnacle Goose *Branta leucopsis*	1980-89 (see Systematic List)
Bar-headed Goose *Anser indicus*	1983-89
Emperor Goose *Anser canagicus*	1985-89
Andean Goose *Chloephaga melanoptera*	1989
Cape Shelduck *Tadorna cana*	1988, 1989
Ruddy Shelduck *Tadorna ferruginea*	1980, 1982, 1983, 1985-88
American Wigeon *Anas americana*	1988
Chiloe Wigeon *Anas sibilatrix*	1983
Cinnamon Teal *A. cyanoptera septentrionalium*	1988
Ringed Teal *Anas leucophrys*	1985, 1986, 1989
Chilean Pintail *Anas spinicauda*	1989
Australian Wood Duck *Chenonetta jubata*	1980, 1985
Wood Duck *Aix sponsa*	1981, 1983-88
Golden Pheasant *Chrysolophus pictus*	1985

Index of English Names

Auk, Little 51
Avocet 32

Bee-eater 54
Bittern 13
   Little 13
Blackbird 63
Blackcap 67
Bluethroat 61
Brambling 73
Bullfinch 77
Bunting, Cirl 77
   Corn 79
   Lapland 77
   Little 78
   Ortolan 78
   Reed 79
   Snow 77
Bustard, Great 31
   Little 31
Buzzard 26
   Honey 24
   Rough-legged 27

Chaffinch 73
Chiffchaff 67
Chough 71
Coot 31
Cormorant 13
Corncrake 31
Courser, Cream-coloured 33
Crake, Spotted 31
Crane 31
Crossbill 76
Crow, Carrion 72
Cuckoo 52
Curlew 42
   Stone 33

Dipper 61
Diver, Black-throated 10
   Great Northern 10
   Red-throated 10
Dotterel 35
Dove, Collared 52
   Stock 52
   Turtle 52
Dowitcher, Long-billed 40
Duck, Australian Wood 80
   Ferruginous 22
   Long-tailed 23
   Ring-necked 21
   Ruddy 24
   Tufted 22
   Wood 80
Dunlin 39
Dunnock 61

Eagle, White-tailed 25
Eider 23

Falcon, Gyr 29
   Red-footed 28
Fieldfare 63
Firecrest 68
Flycatcher, Pied 69
   Red-breasted 69
   Spotted 68
Fulmar 11

Gadwall 18
Gannet 13
Garganey 20
Godwit, Bar-tailed 41
   Black-tailed 41
Goldcrest 68
Goldeneye 23
Goldfinch 73
Goosander 24

81

Goose, Andean 80
　Bar-headed 80
　Barnacle 17, 80
　Bean 80
　Brent 17
　Canada 16
　Egyptian 17
　Emperor 80
　Greylag 16
　Lesser White-fronted 80
　Pink-footed 16, 80
　Snow 80
　White-fronted 16
Goshawk 26
Grebe, Black-necked 11
　Great-crested 11
　Little 10
　Red-necked 11
　Slavonian 11
Greenfinch 73
Greenshank 43
Grouse, Black 29
　Red 29
Guillemot 51
Gull, Black-headed 46
　Common 47
　Glaucous 48
　Great Black-backed 48
　Herring 47
　Iceland 47
　Ivory 49
　Lesser Black-backed 47
　Little 46
　Mediterranean 46
　Ring-billed 47
　Sabine's 46

Harrier, Hen 25
　Marsh 25
　Montagu's 26
Hawfinch 77
Heron, Grey 14
　Night 14

Purple 14
Squacco 14
Hobby 28
Hoopoe 54

Ibis, Glossy 15
　Sacred 80
Jackdaw 71
Jay 71

Kestrel 27
Kingfisher 54
Kite, Black 25
　Red 25
Kittiwake 48
Knot 36

Lapwing 36
Linnet 73

Magpie 71
Mallard 19
Mandarin 18
Martin, House 58
　Sand 58
Merganser, Red-breasted 24
Merlin 28
Moorhen 31

Nightingale 61
Nightjar 54
Nutcracker 71
Nuthatch 70

Oriole, Golden 70
Osprey 27
Ouzel, Ring 63
Owl, Barn 52
　Hawk 53
　Little 53
　Long-eared 53
　Scops 53
　Short-eared 53

82

Owl *continued*
  Snowy 53
  Tawny 53
Oystercatcher 32

Partridge, Grey 29
  Red-legged 29
Peregrine 29
Petrel, Leach's 12
  Storm 12
  Wilson's 12
Phalarope, Grey 45
  Red-necked 45
Pheasant 30
  Golden 80
Pigeon, Wood 52
Pintail 19
  Chilean 80
Pipit, Meadow 59
  Richard's 58
  Rock 59
  Tawny 58
  Tree 59
  Water 59
Plover, Golden 35
  Grey 36
  Kentish 35
  Little Ringed 33
  Ringed 35
Pochard 21
  Red-crested 20
Pratincole, Collared 33
Puffin 52

Quail 29

Rail, Water 30
Raven 72
Razorbill 51
Redpoll 76
Redshank 43
  Spotted 42
Redstart 62

Black 61
Redwing 63
Robin 61
Roller 54
Rook 71
Ruff 39

Sanderling 36
Sandgrouse, Pallas's 52
Sandpiper, Broad-billed 39
  Buff-breasted 39
  Common 44
  Curlew 38
  Green 43
  Pectoral 38
  Purple 39
  Solitary 43
  White-rumped 38
  Wood 44
Scaup 22
Scoter, Common 23
  Velvet 23
Shag 13
Shearwater, Cory's 12
  Manx 12
Shelduck 18
  Cape 80
  Ruddy 17, 80
Shoveler 20
Shrike, Great Grey 71
  Lesser Grey 71
  Red-backed 71
  Woodchat 71
Siskin 73
Skua, Arctic 45
  Great 46
  Long-tailed 45
  Pomarine 45
Skylark 56
Smew 24
Snipe 40
  Great 40
  Jack 40

83

Sparrow, House 72
  Tree 73
Sparrowhawk 26
Spoonbill 15
Starling 72
  Rose-coloured 72
Stilt, Black-winged 32
Stint, Little 37
  Temminck's 37
Stonechat 62
Stork, Black 14
  White 14
Swallow 58
Swan, Bewick's 15
  Black 80
  Mute 15
  Whooper 16
Swift 54
  Alpine 54

Teal 19
  Cinnamon 80
  Ringed 80
Tern, Arctic 50
  Black 51
  Caspian 49
  Common 50
  Little 50
  Roseate 49
  Sandwich 49
  White-winged Black 51
Thrush, Mistle 64
  Song 63
Tit, Bearded 69
  Blue 70
  Coal 69
  Great 70
  Long-tailed 69
  Marsh 69
  Willow 69

Treecreeper 70
Turnstone 44
Twite 76

Wagtail, Grey 59
  Pied 60
  Yellow 59
Warbler, Aquatic 64
  Barred 66
  Cetti's 64
  Dartford 66
  Garden 66
  Grasshopper 64
  Icterine 66
  Marsh 64
  Melodious 66
  Reed 64
  Savi's 64
  Sedge 64
  Yellow-browed 67
  Willow 67
  Wood 67
Waxwing 60
Wheatear 63
Whimbrel 42
Whinchat 62
Whitethroat 66
  Lesser 66
Wigeon 18
  American 80
  Chiloe 80
Woodcock 41
Woodlark 56
Woodpecker, Great Spotted 56
  Green 56
  Lesser Spotted 56
Wren 61
Wryneck 56

Yellowhammer 77